# LIVING YOUR VOCATION

## (EVEN IF YOU DON'T KNOW WHAT IT IS YET)

—

FR NICHOLAS PAUL CROWE, O.P.

All booklets are published
thanks to the generosity of the supporters
of the Catholic Truth Society

First published 2024
by The Incorporated Catholic Truth Society,
42-46 Harleyford Road, London SE11 5AY.
Tel: 020 7640 0042. *www.ctsbooks.org*
© 2024 The Incorporated Catholic Truth Society.
All rights reserved.

ISBN 978 1 78469 766 2

# Contents

# A Gift from God and a Gift to God

When I was a small child, there was a tent at the Christmas fair in my parish. Every item in the tent cost fifty pence. The idea was that a parent could give their child a fifty pence coin, and with that coin the child could secretly choose a Christmas present for their parents. The child would have the joy of 'surprising' their parents with a gift on Christmas Day. The parents would have the joy of receiving a little sign of love from their child.

Of course, the parents organised everything at this Christmas fair: they put up the tent; they filled the tent with suitable items for a child to give as a Christmas present; they took turns to make sure that there was always someone present to supervise and assist the children; they brought their child to the tent, put a fifty-pence coin in the child's hand and explained to the child what they needed to do. Everything about this situation was engineered by the parents so that their children might give them a gift.

Even the gift itself was really for the child's sake, that the child might have the joy and pleasure of presenting their parents with a gift on Christmas Day.

Yet, even so, we intuitively recognise that whatever the child chooses really is the child's gift. It is the child's choice; the gift reflects the child's personality and tastes; it is a sign of the child's love. For this reason, whatever the child chooses is pleasing to the child's parents. The child cannot make a bad choice of gift if they are trying to co-operate in the process. I bought my mother a small and extremely ugly statue of a robin, complete with bulging eyes and a garish red chest. It remains the most successful present I have ever bought my mother. An objectively ugly object was made beautiful by the innocent love with which it was offered.

I want to propose that this tent at my parish Christmas fair is a good analogy for our divine vocation or calling from God. Just as the parents in my parish engineered a situation in which their small children could offer them a gift, so God has created this world so that we might have the joy of offering him a gift. Our life is a gift of love from our heavenly Father: our task is to offer him a gift of love in return as a sign of our gratitude. This is the frame through which to view our vocational choices: we are little children offering our heavenly Father a gift. More important, then, than what we choose is the love with which our gift is offered. Perhaps, objectively speaking, our life might seem unimpressive or even an ugly mess. But if we offer up our life as a gift of love, then our gift will be welcomed with joy. It is by loving that we fulfil our vocation.

# What Is a Vocation?

---

What, then, is a vocation? Our English word 'vocation' comes from the Latin *vocat*, which means 'he or she calls'. When we use this word 'vocation' in a Christian context, it carries the sense of a summons. To have a vocation is to be called or summoned to some definite goal. This means that everyone has a vocation because everyone is summoned to share in the perfect happiness of God in heaven. At this most fundamental level, we all have the same vocation. Yet, we make this journey to the ultimate end of our life by way of acts of charity – that is, by gifts of love offered to God either directly through worship or indirectly through loving our neighbour. Included within God's most fundamental call to share his life in heaven we therefore find a myriad of intermediate calls to love God and neighbour in this life. It is in this secondary sense of a call to intermediate goals that our vocations are different, because in this life God summons us to love in different ways.

This means that, strictly speaking, over the course of a Christian life we will have many vocations according to the different aspects and seasons of our life. Some of our callings are permanent. To be called to Baptism or to Ordination, for example, is to be called into a state that lasts for ever, on account of the sacramental characters that these sacraments confer. Some vocations last only until death: a marriage, for example, is "until death do us part". If our husband or wife dies, then we are free to marry someone else. Other callings are for a season of our life only: we might be called to hold a particular office or take on a particular job or mission for a time and then move on. For example, we might be called to care for an elderly relative in their final years or to work for a particular charity at a difficult moment in their history, but we might not be summoned to do these things forever. Some callings are of an extremely short duration; for example, God in his providential care for creation may be calling you to perform a particular act of mercy and love for someone in need today. One such example is found in the Acts of the Apostles when Ananias was summoned by God to lay his hands on Saul (see *Ac* 9:10-18). This was a real vocation: Ananias was summoned by God to a definite goal, called by God to perform a definite task, and he fulfilled this vocation that same day.

There are many different kinds of vocation, but all, at heart, are an invitation from God to attain some definite end or goal, and by these acts of charity we come to the ultimate end of our life, which is the perfect love and happiness of the vision of God in heaven. This fundamental calling to share God's life in heaven includes within it all the other intermediate calls of our life.

My proposal is that we think of these intermediate calls as our opportunity to offer God a gift. God himself has given us the awesome gift of his friendship and an invitation – a call – to share his happiness forever. An appropriate response to God's gracious generosity is to offer him the gift of our own lives in return, as a sign of our gratitude. Like the parents of the children at my parish Christmas fair, God has prepared everything so that we might have the joy of offering him this gift. Yet the gift is truly our own. In this sign of our gratitude, we journey back to our heavenly Father in union with Christ, and so come to the end to which God calls us in fulfilment of our vocation.

## Problems in vocational discernment

For several years I served as the vocations director for the Dominican friars in Great Britain. During this period, I had the joy of meeting many young men and women who were responding generously to God's call by striving to offer their lives to God as a gift. For many, this ongoing journey of thanksgiving and gift-giving was punctuated (but not exhausted) by a life commitment to serve God and the Church as a priest or through consecrated life or through a particular task or mission. Yet I also met many people for whom the whole question of vocational discernment had become anxiety-ridden, stressful, perhaps even fearful. One man told me that it felt as if he had spent twenty years playing poker with God, desperately trying to 'discern' the cards that God was holding for his life, paralysed by the fear that he would make the 'wrong' decision. This fear is understandable. To choose one path of discipleship is to let go of some of the blessings that make other paths of discipleship so beautiful. This can be a real sacrifice, and sometimes it involves great pain. But if we spend our life at the crossroads, we can never fully offer ourselves to God and neighbour: we cannot fully commit ourselves to two paths simultaneously. More important than the path we choose is the intention with which the gift is offered. God's omnipotence is such that we will never thwart his plan: like the child choosing a gift in the tent, we cannot get it 'wrong' if we are trying to make of our life "a living sacrifice" (*Rm* 12:1), an offering of love given to our heavenly Father.

Other people feel paralysed in their vocational journey for a different reason: they know very well the gift that they would like to offer God, or feel overwhelmingly drawn to offer him, yet they find themselves obstructed or even thwarted. Perhaps the right person to marry has not emerged. Perhaps they have not found a religious order in which they can flourish. Perhaps they have not been accepted for Ordination. Perhaps they find themselves trapped in work that they find unfulfilling or living in circumstances in which they cannot flourish. What do we do if we feel we cannot make our gift? Or if we feel that somehow our gift has not been accepted?

There are no easy answers to these kinds of questions, but sometimes it is helpful to reframe the question itself. This will not be an essay on vocational discernment. Much has already been written on helpful procedures and practices to follow when trying to discern God's call in the particular circumstances of our life.[1] Instead, I hope to expand the horizons of our vocational language in line with the way that the New Testament itself speaks of vocation and calling. It is easy to feel paralysed by the disappointments and trials of this life, but if we lift our head up from the troubles immediately before us to the wide horizon of God's love, we see that, as in Abel's case, our gift has already been accepted (see *Gn* 4:1-16). "We are children of God *now*" (*1 Jn* 3:2). The gifts we bring to the altar are pleasing to God because they are offered through our Lord Jesus Christ in the unity of the Holy Spirit. It is very easy to lose our sense of freedom and joy as children of God if we let the Good News slide

---

[1]  See the CTS booklets at *go.ctsbooks.org/living-your-vocation*.

to the back of our minds and allow ourselves, instead, to be mesmerised by the problems and dissatisfactions that are immediately before us. If we can lift our heads up high once more and allow God's promises to shape our thoughts and give us hope, then we will see that "the Kingdom of God is at hand" (*Mk* 1:15), "nearer to us now than when we first believed" (*Rm* 13:11), and that the narrow way (see *Mt* 7:14) before us will finally become wide and broad for those who run in the way of the Lord's commands.[2] Perhaps in this wider view of God's calling and of his love, we will detect a hitherto unnoticed path forwards in our journey of discipleship in friendship with God.

---

[2] Prologue to the *Rule of St Benedict*.

# The Baptismal Call

---

We have seen that, at the most fundamental level, our calling is to live in God's friendship forever. Indeed, we can think of our vocation as the working out or fulfilment of God's plan for our life. St Paul puts it like this: "And those whom he predestined he also called; and those whom he called he also justified; and those whom he justified he also glorified" (*Rm* 8:30). For St Paul, our calling or vocation is God's execution in time of our predestination. We are, before all else, called to be converted and to turn or return to God's friendship through Baptism or Confession. St Paul says that "those whom he called, he also justified". To be justified is to be reconciled with God through the Spirit who is poured out for the forgiveness of sins and unites us to Jesus as members of his mystical Body the Church. Once we have been restored to God's friendship in this way, our task, at the instigation of the Holy Spirit, is to carry our cross in imitation of Jesus as part of the community of disciples who follow in our Lord's footsteps.

Discipleship means learning from Jesus so that we might live the same kind of life that Jesus lived: a life of radical self-sacrificial love in communion with other believers. This life of ongoing conversion and discipleship should be the primary reference in our minds when we use the word 'vocation'. To be called by God means that we are called to live in friendship with Jesus in this life by living as his disciples, walking in his footsteps in a deepening repentance and conversion that culminates in the perfect love of the vision of God in heaven. This life of growing friendship with God through our Lord Jesus Christ in the Holy Spirit is our baptismal vocation. We know that we are friends of God when we keep his commandments and live the same kind of life that Jesus lived (see *1 Jn* 2:3-6). A life faithful to our baptismal call will be a life that is devoted to God, a life that gives glory to God. As St Paul says, "those whom he justified he also glorified".

When it comes to God, we can think of 'glorifying' as a kind of 'clarifying'.[3] We glorify God when we make his goodness and his love clear, vivid, distinct and visible to others. St Paul teaches us: "So, whether you eat or drink, or whatever you do, do all to the glory of God" (*1 Co* 10:31). According to St Paul, everything we do should in some

---

[3]  Here, I am following St Thomas Aquinas's presentation in his *Summa Theologiae* (2a2ae.132.res) of St Augustine's comment that to be "glorified is the same as to be clarified" (Tract. lxxxii, c, cxiv *On John*).

way make God's goodness and love clear, bright, vivid, visible, radiant. God's glory should be manifest in our lives, such that through us others might be led to praise God and his goodness.

God's glory is most perfectly revealed through the sacred humanity of our Lord Jesus Christ (see *Jn* 1:14). Christ reveals God's glory because he manifests what God's love looks like when embodied in a human life. When we finally come to our journey's end and see God as he really is, we shall become like Christ in love (see *1 Jn* 3:2). In the fire of God's love, we will leave behind once and for all the darkness that so often snares us, because our minds will be flooded with a divine light. Until then, we do not see God's essence clearly. Instead, as Paul puts it, "we see in a mirror dimly" (*1 Co* 13:12). This means that if we are to be transformed by the glory of God revealed to us in Jesus Christ in this life, then we have to actively co-operate in our friendship with God. As the English Dominican friar Gerald Vann once put it, "The way to become like God is to love God; and to love one must learn, and to learn one must look – not just a fleeting glance, a partial awareness, but a long and deep concentration of awareness."[4] In other words, through sustained and attentive contemplation we are led into a

---

[4] Gerald Vann, *The Son's Course: What Is God Like? How Can We Find Out?* (London and Glasgow, Collins Fontana Books, 1959) p. 8.

deeper love of God. We call one who learns in this way a disciple. To be a disciple of Christ is to learn the ways of Truth and Goodness through loving contemplation in prayer, meditation and study. Here we allow God to guide us and empower us, such that our lives might become transparent to the glory of God. "Whether you eat or drink, or whatever you do, do all to the glory of God" (*1 Co* 10:31). In this way, disciples make God's glory clear, vivid and visible for others.

The only way to understand our calling and the meaning and purpose of our life is to turn our eyes away from ourselves and instead look to God: "It is he that made us, and we are his" (*Ps* 100:3). His love brought us into existence, and in him we will learn the unique way in which we have been called to manifest his glory. No one is an accident. No one's life is outside of God's providential care, no matter the mistakes we may fear that we have made. Whatever our circumstances, empowered by the Spirit, in whom we find forgiveness of sins, and united to Christ and his radical self-sacrificing love, we too can give glory to God and so fulfil our most fundamental vocation and arrive at the end to which God summons us: the perfect happiness of heaven.

# The Secondary States

---

We have seen that it is our baptismal call to live in friendship with God in this life so as to enjoy eternal happiness with God in the next. We have also seen that our friendship with God is expressed by a life of ongoing conversion as a disciple, in which we learn from Jesus in order to live like Jesus – doing all things for the glory of God. Even a cursory reading of the New Testament is enough to make clear that embracing our baptismal vocation and a life of discipleship is a very concrete affair. We live out our friendship with God as disciples of Jesus in the midst of the Church and a personalised web of human relationships. To these relationships we bring the unique constellation of gifts, both natural and supernatural, that God has bestowed upon us; the individual circumstances of our life that God in his Providence has willed or at least permitted for us; and what we have made of ourselves through our past choices both good and bad. An important question arises at this point: which environment or context is most likely to help me become a saint? If holiness – a deep love of God – really is my priority, what form of life will best help me, with all my strengths and weaknesses, to attain that goal? What is the best gift I can make of my life to God our loving Father? This brings us to the second dimension of a divine call: what is usually described as our 'state of life' or 'secondary state'. As the Cistercian monk Fr Augustine Roberts points out, broadly speaking we can identify three 'states of life' in the Gospels which roughly correspond to three different ways in which our Lord calls men and women to be his disciples. These three secondary states are the lay state, the consecrated life, and the clerical state which a man enters through the sacrament of Holy Orders.[5]

## The lay state

We read in the Gospels that, on occasion, Jesus summoned men and women to be his disciples and friends, but to do so with their families and in their homes and in their jobs. Martha, Mary and Lazarus, are examples of this kind of call (see *Lk* 10:38-42; *Jn* 11:1-6). These three were clearly very close to Jesus, but they did not follow him around the Holy Land as he preached and performed

---

[5]   Augustine Roberts, OCSO, *Centered on Christ: A Guide to Monastic Profession* (Collegeville, Minnesota, Liturgical Press, 2005) pp. 1-6.

miracles. Instead, they supported him by their love and friendship, and by giving him a place of recuperation and rest.

Another example might be the anonymous benefactor who provided the upper room for the last supper (see *Mk* 14:12-26). This person supported the mission practically by providing Jesus with the resources and the spaces he needed for his work. Others, such as Nicodemus, tried to support Jesus politically (see *Jn* 7:50-52). Others again, such as Joseph of Arimathea, took care of his body after his crucifixion (see *Mt* 27:57). We might also think of the man who was possessed with a legion of demons (see *Mk* 5:1-20). This man was desperate to climb into the boat with Jesus and the other disciples but was told to remain where he was. He went on to preach in the Decapolis region. These people were Jesus's disciples. They loved him, they learned from him, they supported and furthered his mission. They did not, however, follow him in the immediate and direct sense of leaving everything to physically walk in his footsteps. There is, therefore, an invitation in the New Testament, a call, to be a disciple, to be a saint, to offer our lives to God as a gift, but to do so where we are – in our home, with our families, in our work. This is, of course, the beginnings of the call to serve Christ as a lay person. Indeed, after Pentecost, this group of disciples became by far the largest group in the Church (see *Ac* 2:37-41).

When seeking to understand the lay vocation, it is essential to remember that a lay person's life and mission must be a manifestation of the grace of their Baptism. Through our Baptism and faith, we are united to Christ and share in his anointing as Priest, Prophet and King. Priests are mediators between the divine and the human: bridges between the world of the sacred and the world of the profane. In this sense, there is a *priesthood of all the baptised*, because through our Baptism we become united to the sacred humanity of Jesus, who is a divine person. It is the call of every baptised person, then, to be a bridge between Christ and the world. It is the call of every baptised person to offer spiritual sacrifices for the world. Any aspect of our life can be offered up to God as a spiritual sacrifice, as a gift, in thanksgiving to God and in co-operation with God's plan of salvation. In this way we can relate our daily life to God in everything that we do in order that God's glory may shine in us and through us for our own sanctification and the sanctification of others.[6]

Our share in Christ's *prophetic* anointing empowers us to resist evil and to pass on the faith to others, especially our children.[7] In this way the lay disciple is leaven in the dough (*Lk* 13:21), transforming the world from within, shedding light in the darkness by witnessing to Truth,

---

[6] Vatican II, *Lumen Gentium* (1964) 34.

[7] Ibid., 35.

Goodness and Beauty. Some will always be attracted by this witness, whether or not they themselves make the full journey to faith. Others may ridicule this testimony; in these instances, we share in the rejection of Jesus himself, which ultimately led him to the cross.

Finally, the lay vocation is characterised by its share in the *royal anointing* of Christ. The key idea here is governance: via our royal anointing, we are empowered to co-operate in Christ's kingship over the whole of creation. In the first instance, this summons us to master the various desires and inclinations within us, that these may be directed and ordered to true love of God and neighbour.[8] Next, our sharing in Christ's kingship requires us to strive to transfigure in grace our relationships, such that our families, communities and society become ever more characterised by holiness and justice. Also included within this royal anointing is a summons to humanise the world through art, culture, science, and works of kindness and mercy, as well as a responsibility to steward the resources of this world for the benefit of all.[9]

## Distinctions in the lay state

The lay state can, of course, be further sub-divided into those who are married and those who remain single. Space does not allow a full treatment of the theology of

---

[8]  Ibid., 36.

[9]  St John Paul II, *Christifideles Laici* (1988) 14.

the Sacrament of Marriage in this booklet.[10] Suffice to say, for our present purposes, that the Catholic tradition has historically underlined two key 'goods' of Marriage: first, the fulfilment and happiness of both partners in their mutual love for one another; second, the good of raising children.[11] The sacramental bond established when two people marry conforms the union of husband and wife to the union of Christ the bridegroom with his bride the Church. The normal characteristics of natural conjugal love are in this way healed and elevated into an expression of the Kingdom on Earth. On this basis, Pope St John Paul II declared in his post-synodal exhortation *Familiaris Consortio* that Marriage is the "natural setting in which the human person is introduced into the great family of the Church".[12] We must, therefore, assume that the married state normally includes a call to co-operate in God's creative act through the procreation of children, and a call to raise those children in a "school of love" such that the child is able to mature both naturally and spiritually and so realise the fullness of God's plan for their lives.[13]

---

[10] For CTS booklets on the Sacrament of Marriage, see *go.ctsbooks. org/marriage*.

[11] See Augustine's *De Bono Coniugali* 6.6 10.11 and Aquinas's *Summa Contra Gentiles* 3.123. See also Vatican II, *Gaudium et Spes* (1965) 48-52.

[12] St John Paul II, *Familiaris Consortio* (1981), 13-14.

[13] Ibid., 3.

When it comes to the lay single life, we need to acknowledge that there are many disciples of Christ who find themselves living out their friendship with God alone, and that many of these found themselves on this path without having chosen it. Luanne D. Zurio suggests in her 2019 book *Single for a Greater Purpose*[14] that to ask whether it is God's permissive or active will that so many disciples in the Catholic West are single is not necessarily a helpful question.[15] Instead, we should emphasise that our most important calling is the summons to live in friendship with God in this life so as to enjoy eternal happiness with God in the next. Whatever our circumstances, we are called to love and serve God in this context. We must, then, accept the circumstances in which we find ourselves and look for opportunities to grow in charity in this environment. Notice that accepting our present circumstances does not necessarily mean that we intend these circumstances to become permanent, although they may become so. It simply means that we surrender to the present, confident that our life is not meaningless or an accident. God has called us by name into his friendship. We are destined to spend eternity in the perfect happiness of his love in heaven. If God

---

[14]  Luanne D. Zurio, *Single for a Greater Purpose: A Hidden Joy in the Catholic Church* (Manchester, New Hampshire, Sophia Institute Press, 2019).

[15]  Ibid., p. 6.

has permitted difficulties or disappointments in our life, then with his help there must be an opportunity to make something beautiful of these sufferings by love.

Zurio suggests that there are reasons to think that at this moment in history the witness of single lay disciples is especially important and necessary.[16] The scandals that have rocked the Church in recent decades have, in the eyes of many, discredited the witness of those more closely associated with the institutional Church, such as priests and religious. It may be that lay disciples are better placed to rebuild connections with a mistrustful world and lead it back to Christ. It may be that the complexity of modern society and the speed of societal change is too much for many of the Church's existing structures of mission, and that lay disciples are needed to respond quickly to emerging trends with a spontaneity and expertise that existing institutions would find difficult to match. It may be that single lay people, free from the weight of the institutional and administrative burdens carried by younger clergy and religious in the West, are better positioned to lead the Church's mission to some of the most pressing new frontiers.

Zurio uses the term "Dedicated Single" to signify a lay disciple who has chosen to embrace the opportunities for discipleship inherent in being a single lay disciple in order

---

[16]  Ibid., pp. 143-147.

to love and serve God and the Church wholeheartedly.[17] She also acknowledges that the lack of public recognition or affirmation of this choice can be painful, and that many dedicated single people feel a powerful absence: the restlessness of those who have not found a place of belonging, like "the Son of Man [who] has nowhere to lay his head" (*Mt* 8:20). Yet there is also a hidden joy where our human weakness encounters the power of God (see *2 Co* 12:5-10). Zurio affirms that we are hardwired to give ourselves away, or to use the language that I have been using in this booklet, to make a gift of ourselves to God. Rather than focus on what we do not have, the path to holiness and fulfilment is to focus on the extraordinary opportunity we have been given to make an offering of our lives to God in Christ, to offer ourselves up "as a living sacrifice" (*Rm* 12:1).

## The consecrated life

We have seen that one context in which we might live out our baptismal call is the lay state, the call to serve Jesus and support his mission in the context of our families and our careers. Another kind of call found in the Gospels was to men and women who were invited by Jesus to follow him in a more direct sense on his journeys around the Holy Land, men and women who were invited to give

---

[17] Ibid., pp. 31-49.

up their family life, to give up their jobs and to leave their possessions in order to go where Jesus went. These men and women were summoned to listen to Jesus for longer and more attentively, to work alongside him, to share his life more intensely. One group who were called to follow Jesus in this way were the seventy-two sent out ahead of the Lord to proclaim the Kingdom of God (see *Lk* 10:1-12); another, the women who walked with Jesus and took care of his needs (see *Mk* 15:41). We see in this second kind of call a second way of being a disciple, the beginnings of the consecrated life.[18]

Like the lay disciple, the consecrated man or woman is seeking perfection in charity. Lay people and consecrated people are on the same journey, they are simply on different roads. The main difference is that the structure of a consecrated life should itself be an education in the meaning of the Gospel. The great rules of life of the Catholic tradition such as the *Rule of St Benedict* or the *Rule of St Augustine* embed Christ's teaching into a way of living. If a consecrated man or woman is faithful to their way of life, the life itself will be an education and an immersion in the Gospel that helps us to place Christ at the centre of everything we are and everything we do. Everything in a consecrated life should remind us of God and lead us back to God.

---

[18] Again, see Roberts, *Centered on Christ*, 1-6.

This is why the consecrated life has at its foundation a total dedication to God according to the three evangelical counsels, or guides for Gospel living: poverty, chastity and obedience. On one level, we can think of these counsels as tools that help us to clear the road of obstacles that might hinder our life of discipleship. This is why older books on the religious life[19] will sometimes describe this calling as a "higher way" or as "the way of perfection". This language is less common now because it was so widely misunderstood; nevertheless, it does accurately describe the distinction between the lay state of life and the consecrated state of life.

On one level, the religious life is a higher way in broadly the same way that we describe some roads as being 'highways'. The highway is straight and wide, so that we can drive fast. We could make the same journey via country roads, and this may in fact be a more pleasant drive, but there is a higher chance that something might hold us up on a B road that is not necessarily our fault. There might be a tractor slowing down the traffic, for example, or a cow blocking the road. There might be narrow lanes and blind turns that increase the chance of collision. The highway, in theory, is an easier road, on

---

[19] Religious life is the most well-known form of consecrated life. It involves a community of monks, nuns, friars or sisters living together under a rule.

which we can drive fast.[20] If our aim is to make rapid progress towards our final destination, then the highway is our best bet.

However, as writers such as St Thomas Aquinas remind us, the fact that someone is on "the way of perfection" or "the higher way" as a religious tells us nothing about their personal holiness. We all know that we can be on a highway without making any progress. Many religious men and women are wasting the tools that their way of life places at their disposal. To stretch the analogy to breaking point, rather than progressing in their journey of discipleship, many consecrated men and women are wasting their time in service stations drinking coffee or reading the newspaper. Worse, many are driving fast in the wrong direction. As Aquinas notes, there are many in the lay state who have attained a greater holiness – that is, grown more in charity through perseverance and so come closer to their ultimate end – than many religious brothers and sisters who have been given a more direct road.[21]

Nevertheless, for those who use the tools well and want to persevere on their journey of discipleship, the consecrated life should be a more direct route with less

---

[20] This analogy works less well among those familiar with British motorways.

[21] See St Thomas Aquinas, *De Perfectione,* 18.

distractions. This is not to say that the consecrated life is easy. In this world, growing in charity means taking up our cross daily in imitation of Jesus. In concrete terms, the clearing of obstacles to discipleship means removing some of the ways we might hide from the cross and the painful demands of Christlike love. Yet, paradoxically, the difficulties of the consecrated life are also the mechanisms by which we are led to grow in charity. They force us to confront our difficulty in loving God and neighbour, and focus us on the highest good, which is God himself.

An obvious question arises at this point. A lay disciple who is single abstains from sexual acts at least until they are married. They may voluntarily choose to be poor for the sake of the Kingdom. They will be obedient to the teachings of the Church and perhaps even a rule of life. Indeed, it is clear that the evangelical counsels of poverty, chastity and obedience are proposed by Christ to *all* Christians as a way of facilitating their journey of discipleship, not just a select few. All Christians are encouraged to be poor, chaste and obedient in a manner that is appropriate to their state of life. What is the difference, then, between a single lay person who has voluntarily decided to practise the evangelical counsels in their life of discipleship and a consecrated man or woman who has publicly embraced the life of the counsels?

The answer lies both in the totality of the gift offered by the individual in question and in the divine response.[22] First, the consecrated person offers up their whole selves: they offer up everything they own or have in the promise of poverty not just for a season of their lives but for their whole life. They offer up their bodies to God's praise and service in the promise of celibacy not just for a season of their life but for their whole life. They offer up their wills to God in the promise of obedience not just for a season of their life but for their whole life. The consecrated person makes a total offering of self to God: not just everything they are or have today, but everything they will be or have in the future. The consecrated person gives themselves totally to God.

In being totally given to God, not in part but wholly, a consecrated person is totally set aside for God by God. This is one of the reasons why the Church must confirm new forms of consecrated life. It must be discerned whether this form of dedication is one that God wills and consecrates. If, then, the vocational sphere of the lay person is the world and a summons to be leaven in the dough and salt of the earth (see *Lk* 13:21; *Mt* 5:13), transforming the world from within, the vocational sphere

---

[22] See the excellent theological exploration of the consecrated life offered by Basil Cole and Paul Conner in *Christian Totality: Theology of the Consecrated Life* (New York, Alba House, 1997) and chapter 1 of St Thomas Aquinas's *Apology for the Religious Orders,* also known as the *Contra Retrahentes.*

of the consecrated person is the Kingdom of Heaven. The consecrated person has been set aside by God to manifest the life of heaven here on Earth.

## *The charisms of religious orders*

Just as we could subdivide the lay vocation into a married state and a single state, so we can subdivide the call to consecrated life, and especially the call to enter a religious order. When Jesus says to particular men and women: "Come follow me", he is asking them to live like him and with him. He is asking them to visibly extend his presence and mission over space and time. However, this summons to extend or re-present the life and work of Jesus to the world is impossible for any one individual. It is a mission – a call – that we take on as an entire Church: lay people, consecrated men and women, and clergy. The call to leave everything in order to follow Jesus as a consecrated person must therefore be a call to a particular kind of ecclesial discipleship, a particular pattern of life that represents to the world a particular aspect of Jesus's life and ministry as part of Christ's body the Church.

For example, enclosed monks or nuns on top of a mountain or in the desert re-present to the world the Christ who went up the mountain or into the desert to pray. The Franciscans are called to re-present to the world the poverty of Christ and his compassion for the poor. The Dominicans, the Order of Preachers, are called to re-present to the world the Christ who preached and the Christ who taught. Religious orders are distinguished by their purpose: they re-present different aspects of Jesus's life and mission as one part of the broader mission of the Church. We must never have a competitive model of vocation or calling in our mind. The Church is the body of Christ. She has many members, each called to play their part in establishing the Kingdom of Heaven on Earth. When one part of the Church flourishes, we all benefit. When we praise one vocation or charism, we honour all, because we are members of the same body.

## Ordination

So far, we have seen that the lay state is one context in which our baptismal call to live in friendship with God as disciples is lived out. This state is a call to be leaven in the dough, to transform the world from within. We have also explored a second call to discipleship, the call to leave everything to follow Jesus in the direct sense of leaving home and career in order to live the same kind of life that Jesus lived. This is the root of the consecrated life, the call to be a sign of the Kingdom of Heaven on Earth. This brings us to the third and final mode of discipleship found in the New Testament: the call to Ordination and the clerical state.

From a larger group of disciples Jesus chose twelve whom he named apostles (see *Lk* 6:12-13). These twelve were so powerfully conformed by grace to Christ the head of his body the Church that they could act sacramentally in his person. In this way, the apostles were so configured to Christ that they would become the centre and the source of unity of the body of Christ on Earth after the resurrection. As Jesus had been the centre of the community of disciples during his Earthly ministry, so the apostles were at the centre of the early Church. Bishops are the successors of the apostles. As such, a bishop stands at the centre of his diocese through the grace of Holy Orders as the point of unity with the universal Church.[23]

Bishops are first of all called to the sacred ministry of Christ in Word and Sacrament. They offer a guaranteed and authoritative mediation between God and his people. This means that bishops are called to re-present to the world not just an aspect of Christ's ministry, as with the charism of a religious order, for example, but the whole Christ. This is, of course, impossible at a personal level, but by the grace of Ordination a bishop is able to act in the person of Christ sacramentally. As such, the bishop represents the fullness of the priesthood. A priest is a limb or extension of the bishop; the deacon is a representative of the bishop.[24]

---

[23] Again, see Roberts, *Centered on Christ,* 1-6.

[24] Second Vatican Council, *Lumen Gentium*, 18-29.

There is a sense, then, that the parish priest, as a limb of the bishop, is called to represent Christ in a more holistic way than a non-ordained consecrated person. Where the religious brother or sister re-presents particular aspects of Jesus's life and ministry, the parish priest when acting in Christ's person re-presents the whole Christ, and this wholeness spills out into his entire ministry. A parish priest must, as St Paul puts it, be all things to all men and women in order to win some of them for Christ (see *1 Co* 9:22). The parish priest has the responsibility to care for his flock, whoever they may be and, to a certain extent, whatever they may throw at him. His task is to preach, sanctify and govern under the authority of the bishop in whose ministry he participates.

Space does not allow a fuller treatment of the riches of the grace of Ordination.[25] Suffice to say that the requisites on the part of a man proposed for Ordination are a good intention, a firm resolve and the capacity to bear the burdens of the priestly life. These three criteria are drawn from a letter composed by Cardinal Merry del Val in 1912 in response to a dispute in France over the signs of a priestly vocation. The letter was approved by Pope St Pius X and published in *Acta Apostolicae Sedis V* the following year.[26] By "a good intention" we

---

[25] For a fuller exploration of the call to the priesthood, see the CTS booklets at *go.ctsbooks.org/priesthood*.

[26] *Acta Apostolicae Sedis V* (1913) 290.

mean that a man offers himself for the priesthood for the right reasons – that is, he wishes to offer his life as a gift to God and God's people in and through the sacred ministry. By "a firm resolve" we mean more than a passing whimsy but rather a firm and stable act of will to make and persevere in this offering. By "capacity" we simply mean the natural, moral and supernatural personal attributes needed to shepherd God's flock in the name of the Good Shepherd himself. It belongs to the bishop to confirm a man's sense of calling and judge him an appropriate candidate for Ordination on the basis of his personal qualities, his circumstances and his preparation.

# God's Call for Me Today

---

We have now explored two dimensions of a divine vocation: first, our baptismal call to friendship with God and a life of discipleship that culminates in the perfect happiness of heaven and, second, the anchoring of this call to discipleship in a particular network of relationships through embracing a particular state of life within the Church. The third and final dimension of our vocation is even more specific. It refers to the day-to-day reality of living as a disciple in this time and in this place. What, concretely, is God asking of me today? As the psalmist sings, "O that today you would listen to his voice" (*Ps* 95:7).

This third dimension of our calling embraces both our personal and our professional lives, as well as our natural and supernatural gifts. It is inherently the most fluid: unlike the calls to Baptism or Ordination, which impart a permanent sacramental character, or religious consecration and Marriage, which are commitments that endure until death, this third dimension of our calling might only apply to a season of our life or even to one particular moment. The world does not stand still, and neither do we. As we move through life, we find that our circumstances and our relationships change, and so Christ's New Law of love makes new demands on us. We cannot, then, think of our vocation as being something static. It does not matter whether we are at the end of our journey with Christ or at the beginning: each day we must open our ears as disciples (see *Is* 50:4) and resist the hardness of heart (see *Ps* 95:1-11; *Heb* 3:11) that deflects God's call. Each and every day, we are called to a deepening love of God and neighbour. Each and every day, we must renew our gift once more: offering up our life in whatever context we find ourselves as a gift of love to our Father in heaven.

## A Christian attitude to work

With this in mind, it is important to consider the role that work plays in our Christian calling. Much of what we do on any given day is work. Be it employed work, volunteering work or work at home, most of us spend a significant proportion of our time working, and much of this work is unglamorous. Yet, whilst much of our work might seem mundane, work that is good can always be offered up as part of our gift to God and as a co-operation in his providential care for the world. The role of human work in God's providential care of creation has been insightfully explored in recent years by the presbyterian minister Tim Keller.[27] Keller notes that if we turn to a biblical text such as Psalm 147 (146), we find the psalmist praising God for works that only God – in the biblical imagination – could do. For example, God is praised for determining "the number of the stars" (*Ps* 147:4), for making "grass grow upon the hills" (*Ps* 147:8) and so on. Yet in the same psalm, God is also praised for work that human beings do. For example, God is praised for strengthening the bars of the city gates, making peace within Israel's borders and filling the people with finest wheat (see *Ps* 147:13-14). But as Keller points out, the people we actually see strengthening the bars of the city gates are carpenters and builders and other such workmen. The people we actually see maintaining peace within a nation's borders are the police and all those entrusted with the responsibility of maintaining law and order. The people we actually see satisfying us with finest wheat are the farmers, the HGV drivers, the bakers, the people that work in the supermarkets, everyone involved in making sure that we are provided with a loaf of bread when we pop into a shop on our way home from work. Yet God gets the credit for all of this human work.[28]

---

[27] Timothy Keller and Katherine Leary Alsdorf, *Every Good Endeavor: Connecting Your Work to God's Plan for the World* (London, Hodder and Stoughton, 2012).

[28] Keller and Alsdorf, *Every Good Endeavor*, pp. 68-71.

Keller's key insight here is that if God is being praised for the work of ordinary people going about their lives, then this must mean that ordinary work is or can be the work of God. As Catholic thinkers such as St Thomas Aquinas have long understood, God is praised for the work of human hands because God holds every creature in being at every moment. God is the primary cause of all that happens in our world: he is the cause even of our free human actions. God's omnipotence and omniscience are such that he is able to work out his plan of salvation in our world in and through genuinely free human choices. All of us are instruments of God. He uses even our mistakes to further his purposes. But if our deeds are good, and we knowingly and willingly offer up our work to God as a gift, then we become loving co-operators in God's providential care for his creatures.[29]

We noted above that consecrated men and women are called to 're-present' some aspect of Christ's ministry to this time and this place, and that ordained ministers, as limbs of the bishop, have an even more holistic calling to represent Christ the head, especially when ministering the sacraments. Against this backdrop, it is easy to see how the work of a priest or a religious might be the work of God. Yet it is important to emphasise that our co-operation with the work of God extends far beyond

---

[29] St Thomas Aquinas, *Summa Theologiae*, 1a.22-26.

'churchy' roles. If our work is somehow providing for the needs of God's children, if our work is somehow making another person's life better, then we are, or can be, part of God's providential care for that person. More than this, if we do our work with love, our work can become part of the way that we offer ourselves as a gift of love to God.

This idea has some dramatic implications for the way that we see the world. It means that all the people around us doing their jobs well are God's gift to us. In our turn, we are God's gift to them. To use some direct examples inspired by the writing of Tim Keller, the plumber who comes round to unblock your sink is a gift to you from God. Through him, God is looking after you. The people who have made sure that we are able to eat today are co-operating in God's nourishment of his children. The people who clean your office or clean your hall of residence are also God's gift to you: they are helping to make your life just a bit more comfortable, a bit more bearable. The teachers who educate us, the doctors and nurses who keep us healthy, the construction workers who provide us with shelter – all these people in different ways are part of God's nurturing of his children. If our work is good work, if our work is just, then we too can be a gift from God to other people. We too can become a reason for others to thank God.[30]

---

[30] Keller and Alsdorf, *Every Good Endeavor*, pp. 71-80.

But what if I find it difficult to see how my work benefits other people? The world has become very complex. A global economy can be morally ambiguous, and in an increasingly environmentally conscious age these ambiguities seem only to be deepening. It may well be difficult to see how we are co-operating with God's providential care of his people in the world. It may not be clear that the system we are embroiled in is in fact good and worthwhile and contributing to the well-being of society. It may not be clear what we need to do in order to fix the problem. It may not seem possible, given my circumstances, to change careers in order to take work that is more obviously worthwhile.

I would suggest that if a job is obviously immoral a Catholic should be seeking employment elsewhere. In situations that are more ambiguous or complicated, the minimum required of us is justice. By 'justice' we mean giving to each person what they are owed, giving to each person their due as human beings loved by God and made in his image and likeness. The demands of justice may well summon us to work step-by-step for the transformation of our industry, our community or our world. Whilst God has permitted the economic, social and political environment in which we find ourselves, this does not necessarily mean that he willed the arrangements under which we live. In other words, we cannot assume that the existing political and economic order is what God intended. Instead, it is part of our Christian calling to strive day-by-day for the re-ordering of the systems in which we live and work towards Truth, Goodness and Beauty. Even if the best we can achieve are small gestures and small acts of kindness, it is our calling to humanise our work in order to protect the dignity of every person. This is especially true for those in the lay state, those called to be leaven in the dough, transforming the world from within. If this seems like a daunting – if not outright impossible – task, we must remember that nothing is impossible to God. The difficulty inherent in the task is what makes it such a powerful tool of moral and spiritual transformation.

## Love, and do what you will

I think it is fair to say that in the Church's contemporary vocational discourse this third level of daily fidelity to the call of Christ is the most neglected. There can be a tendency to focus excessively on the question of our state of life to the exclusion of all else. Yet our baptismal call to live in friendship with God as his disciples is more fundamental, and we live out this call in a daily fidelity to the summons of love in whatever situation we find ourselves. If we are forgetful of this daily summons from God to lay down our life (see *Lk* 9:23) in charity, we risk a blindness towards opportunities to offer gifts of love to God here and now; we risk wasting gifts, talents and expertise that have been given for the building up of the Kingdom of God on Earth; and we risk making bad choices when it comes to the second dimension of our calling, our state of life.

My instinct is that if people take their baptismal vocation seriously and persevere in that journey in a daily fidelity to the call of divine charity, then the second level of their vocation – the question whether to choose the priesthood, the life of a consecrated person, Marriage or the single lay life – will largely look after itself. My idea is not original or complicated; it is simply that if people get today right, tomorrow will work itself out. If we are in the right place today, we are more likely to find our way, a little further down the road, to the right place tomorrow. If we are focused – every day – on loving God and translating that love into action as faithful disciples, then we can trust our instincts when it comes to a decision about our state of life.

St Augustine famously declared "Love, and do what you will."[31] This quotation has been much abused, but in essence St Augustine is teaching that all our good deeds begin in the grace of God. We love because God loved us first (see *1 Jn* 4:11). In loving us, he gives us the desire to love him in return. God calls us through an internal

---

[31] St Augustine, *Homilies on the First Epistle of John,* Homily 7 (*1 Jn* 4:4-12), paragraph 8.

movement of the Holy Spirit, who instigates a free choice on our part to offer God a gift. Being guided and moved by the Spirit is not an alternative to rational judgement. On the contrary, the Spirit expands our freedom and strengthens our powers to choose well. Even in those cases where a private revelation makes a call explicit, for example when Paul was knocked off his horse on the road to Damascus (see *Ac* 9:1-9), or when Paul and Barnabus are set apart by the Spirit for the work to which they had been called (*Ac* 13:2), there is still a choice to be made under the impetus of an internal grace to accept this summons. This choice to freely offer the gift that God instigates in us is one that resonates with our highest desires, our deepest loves. The Spirit gives us access to our best self. God calls us through desires and loves that he himself wrote into our nature at the moment of our creation and perfected in his gifts of grace. We can love and do what we will because if we are truly loving then we are being moved by a love that comes from God.

## Recognising God's call

The gifts we offer God are, therefore, those that he himself moves us to make because God loves us first. Like the parents in my parish at the Christmas fair,[32] God has organised everything so that we, his children,

---

[32] See the first chapter in this booklet.

might offer him a gift, even to the point of instigating these acts of love and devotion in our hearts. Yet the gift remains truly our own. God moves us in a manner that in no way competes with our freedom. Instead, God's grace enhances our freedom by elevating our intellect and will, such that we can choose in a manner that resonates with our own deepest desires.

We facilitate our co-operation with the work of the Spirt in our lives through a commitment to the spiritual disciplines of prayer, fasting and almsgiving, as well as the intellectual discipline of meditating on God's Word under the guidance of the teachings of the Church. According to St Thomas Aquinas, the "New Law" promulgated by Christ in his Sermon on the Mount is a "law of the Holy Spirit".[33] This New Law of the Holy Spirit is, in the first place, unwritten. That is, it is written in the first place directly onto the human heart. As we have already noted, the Spirit guides our life through the elevation of our intellect and will, such that we can more easily grasp what is most important in any given situation and will what is most precious. Unlike the old law which moved us from without but could not heal the damage of sin, the New Law of the Holy Spirit moves us from within in accord with desires and inclinations that God himself has placed in our heart.

---

[33] St Thomas Aquinas, *Summa Theologiae*, 1a.2ae.106, 107, 108.

In a secondary sense, however, the New Law is written. Through the Scriptures, written by human authors but inspired by the Holy Spirit, we encounter the holy teaching of our Lord Jesus. Christ unfolds for us what it means to live in friendship with God in this life so as to enjoy eternal happiness with him forever in the next. He shows us both what we should be aiming for in this life and how we get there. He reveals to us the kinds of lives and the kinds of offerings that are pleasing to God. If we are striving to understand God's call for our life in any sphere, then we must pay close attention to our Lord's teaching in the Scriptures. As the voice of the Father declared from the cloud at the Transfiguration: "This is my beloved Son, listen to Him" (*Mk* 9:7). It is hard to discern, if we do not know what we should be aiming for or how to get there. We have to meditate on the holy teaching of Jesus.

The written and unwritten elements of the New Law can never be in contradiction, as both are inspired by the same Spirit. Indeed, the internal prompting of the Spirit is meant to guide us in our application of Scripture, such that a spiritual person is able to apply appropriately the general principles that they find in the Scriptures, as interpreted by the Church, to their own concrete circumstances. St Paul teaches us that "all who are led by the Spirit of God are children of God" (*Rm* 8:14). The spiritual person begins to share God's perspective on creation: she gains a more profound insight into God's providential ordering of her life; she grasps more clearly what the teaching of Jesus aims to achieve and how it might be implemented in her own circumstances. As a child of God whose mind has been renewed by the grace of the Holy Spirit, she acquires a taste for God's holy wisdom and an instinct for his will. This is why the basic tools of the spiritual life – the sacraments, prayer, fasting and almsgiving – are so essential if we are to be docile to the Spirit and offer gifts pleasing to God. They foster a sensitivity to the Spirit, such that we can more readily apply the teachings of Christ to our own situation and offer up to God a gift that is appropriate to both our natural and our supernatural gifts, as well as the context in which we find ourselves.

These same intellectual and spiritual disciplines lay a foundation for the undoing, under the Spirit's guidance and strength, of the imprint of sin in our life. The legacy of our own sins, and the impact upon us of other people's sins, can have a disordering impact on our desires and appetites. To put it very simply, when Augustine declares "Love and do what you will", he is referring to our highest loves, what our best self loves, the inclinations written into our nature by God and later perfected in grace to which the Spirit gives us access. But these holy desires can be clouded or obscured by disordered passions pulling us in other directions. I can love the wrong things or become attached to good things in a disproportionate manner, in such a way that my appetites and desires become confused and it becomes much more difficult both to recognise in myself a holy desire to offer a gift to God and to persevere in that gift. This internal confusion can make the Christian life unnecessarily anxious and painful, perhaps even joyless.

Christ came to set us free from the oppressive touch of sin in our world. He came to call sinners and give us new life. Even in the midst of the confusing passions and appetites, we can turn to God who preserves our freedom. For "where sin increased, grace abounded all the more" (*Rm* 5:20), and "he will not let you be tempted beyond your strength" (*1 Co* 10:13). The healing and elevating power of the Spirit preserves our freedom to choose well, to offer our gift, even if it is more difficult in the midst of struggle and temptation. Over time, through a daily fidelity to our baptismal call, the struggle lessens, and by the grace of God the sphere of our freedom expands. We find healing and integration. Our vocational confusion diminishes. We find the peace of God, even when we find ourselves in circumstances that we have not chosen. We can offer our gift with joy.

# Concluding Thoughts

I began this booklet by proposing the image of a small child offering a gift to their parents as a frame through which to understand our vocational journey. We are God's children, and we are invited to share God's happiness in heaven forever. This, at the most fundamental level, is our vocation: the definite end to which God summons us. The appropriate response to the great gift of God's love and friendship is to offer him a gift in return as a sign of our gratitude and thanksgiving. This is our baptismal vocation: we lay down our lives as disciples following Christ in a journey characterised by ongoing conversion and deepening love. Ordinarily, this journey includes a commitment to a particular mode of discipleship, be it lay, consecrated or ordained. Here, we commit to loving, serving and honouring God in a particular mode: as a priest, as a consecrated person, through our marriage, as a lay disciple. This commitment to a particular state of life within the Church shapes and conditions the rest of our journey. Day by day, we are called to open our ears as disciples and take up our cross in love in a manner appropriate to our state of life and our circumstances. Daily fidelity to God's call leads us to an appropriate life commitment as we nurture an ever-deeper sensitivity to the prompting of the Holy Spirit. Daily fidelity to God's call disposes us to grow in charity and thereby sustains these life commitments and allows the gift we offer to God to be sustained for a lifetime. In daily fidelity we grow in holiness, and so this daily fidelity is obedience to our vocation in the fullest sense, for the charity in our hearts today is already a participation in the perfect love of heaven.

# Bibliography

This short bibliography includes only texts that have been used in this booklet. Biblical texts were taken from the Revised Standard Version due to its ease of online access.

St Thomas Aquinas (original Latin text taken from the Aquinas Institute's 'aquinas.cc' online tool (*aquinas.cc*); all translations are from the original Latin and are my own):

– *Contra Retrahentes*
– *De Perfectione*
– *Summa Contra Gentiles*
– *Summa Theologiae.*

St Augustine of Hippo (texts for whose writings can be found online at *https://www.newadvent.org/fathers/*):

– *De Bono Coniugali* (*On the Good of Marriage*)

– Homily 7, *Homilies on the First Epistle of John.*

St Benedict of Nursia, *The Rule of St Benedict*, Timothy Fry, trans. (Collegeville, Liturgical Press, 1981).

St John Paul II, *Christifideles Laici*, 30th December 1988. *www.vatican.va/content/john-paul-ii/en/apost_exhortations/ documents/hf_jp-ii_exh_30121988_christifideles-laici.html.*

St John Paul II, *Familiaris Consortio*, 22nd November 1981. *www.vatican.va/content/john-paul-ii/en/apost_exhortations/ documents/hf_jp-ii_exh_19811122_familiaris-consortio.html.*

Vatican II, *Gaudium et Spes* (Pastoral Constitution on the Church in the Modern World) 7th December 1965, in *Vatican II: The Conciliar and Postconciliar Documents*, General Editor, Austin Flannery OP (Leominster, Fowler Wright Books Ltd. 1981) pp. 903-1002.

Vatican II, *Lumen Gentium* (Dogmatic Constitution on the Church) 21st November 1964, in *Vatican II: The Conciliar and Postconciliar Documents*, General Editor, Austin Flannery OP (Leominster, Fowler Wright Books, 1981) pp. 350-426.

Cole, Basil, and Conner, Paul. *Christian Totality: Theology of the Consecrated Life* (New York, Alba House, 1997).

Keller, Timothy, and Alsdorf, Katherine Leary. *Every Good Endeavor: Connecting Your Work to God's Plan for the World* (London, Hodder and Stoughton, 2012).

Roberts, Augustine. *Centered on Christ: A Guide to Monastic Profession* (Collegeville, Minnesota, Liturgical Press, 2005).

Vann, Gerald. *The Son's Course: What Is God Like? How Can We Find Out?* (London and Glasgow, Collins Fontana Books, 1959).

Zurio, Luanne D. *Single for a Greater Purpose: A Hidden Joy in the Catholic Church* (Manchester, New Hampshire, Sophia Institute Press, 2019).